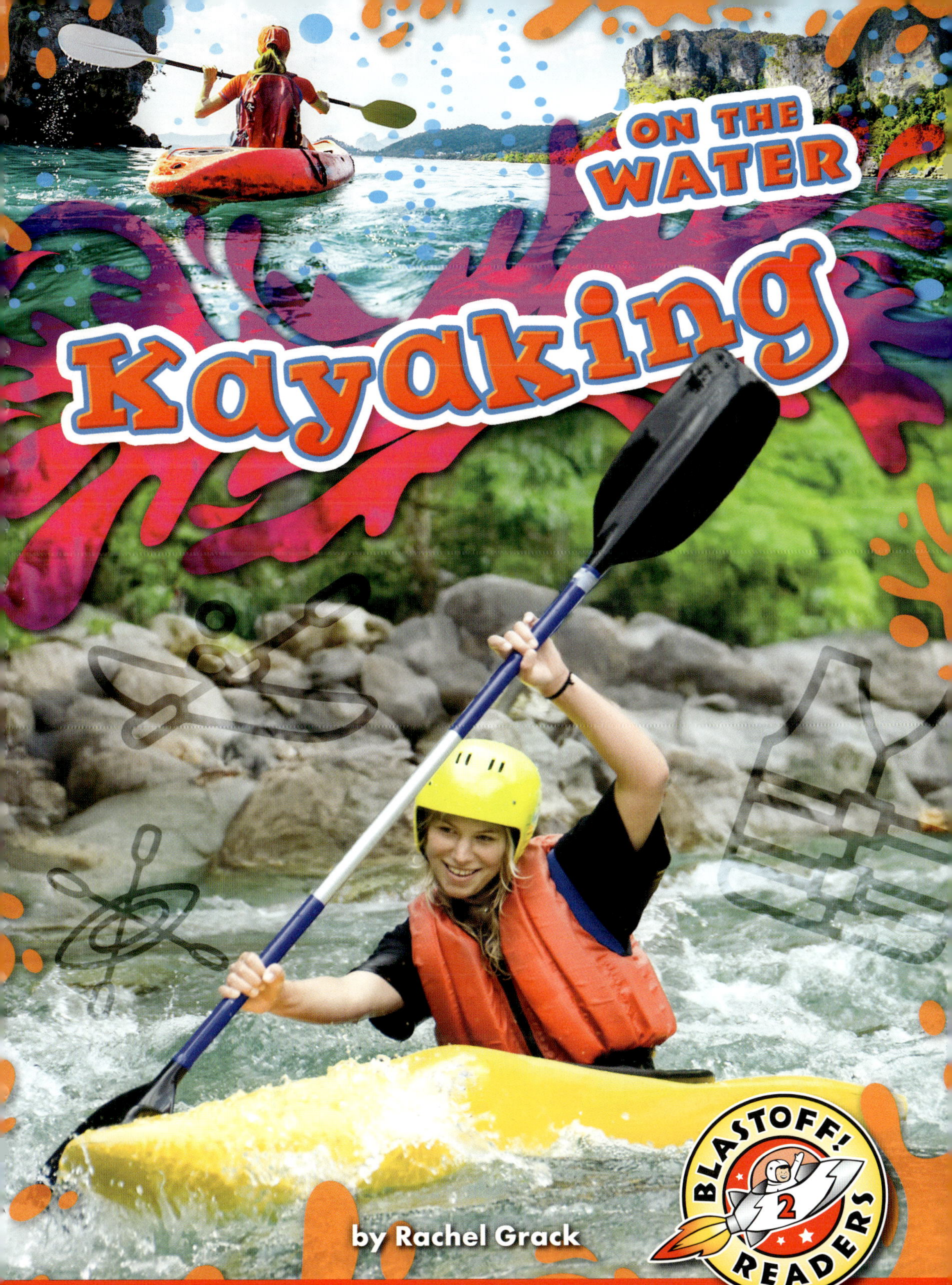

ON THE WATER

Kayaking

by Rachel Grack

BLASTOFF! 2 READERS

BLASTOFF! READERS, AN IMPRINT OF BELLWETHER MEDIA BY FLUTTERBEE

Blastoff! Readers are carefully developed by literacy experts to build reading stamina and move students toward fluency by combining standards-based content with developmentally appropriate text.

Level 1 provides the most support through repetition of high-frequency words, light text, predictable sentence patterns, and strong visual support.

Level 2 offers early readers a bit more challenge through varied sentences, increased text load, and text-supportive special features.

Level 3 advances early-fluent readers toward fluency through increased text load, less reliance on photos, advancing concepts, longer sentences, and more complex special features.

★ **Blastoff! Universe**

This edition first published in 2027 by Bellwether Media, Inc.

For information regarding permission, write to Bellwether Media, Inc., Attention: Permissions Department, 3500 American Blvd W, Suite 150, Bloomington, MN 55431.

Library of Congress Cataloging-in-Publication Data is available at www.loc.gov or upon request from the publisher.

ISBN: 9798898800574 (hardcover)
ISBN: 9798898801816 (ebook)

Editor: Kieran Downs Designer: Josh Brink

Printed in the United States of America, North Mankato, MN.

Table of Contents

All About Kayaking

Kayaks are small, narrow boats. They have a pointed **bow** and **stern**.

People enjoy kayaking on lakes, rivers, and oceans. It is a popular water sport.

Top Place to Kayak

Boundary Waters Canoe Area Wilderness, Minnesota, United States

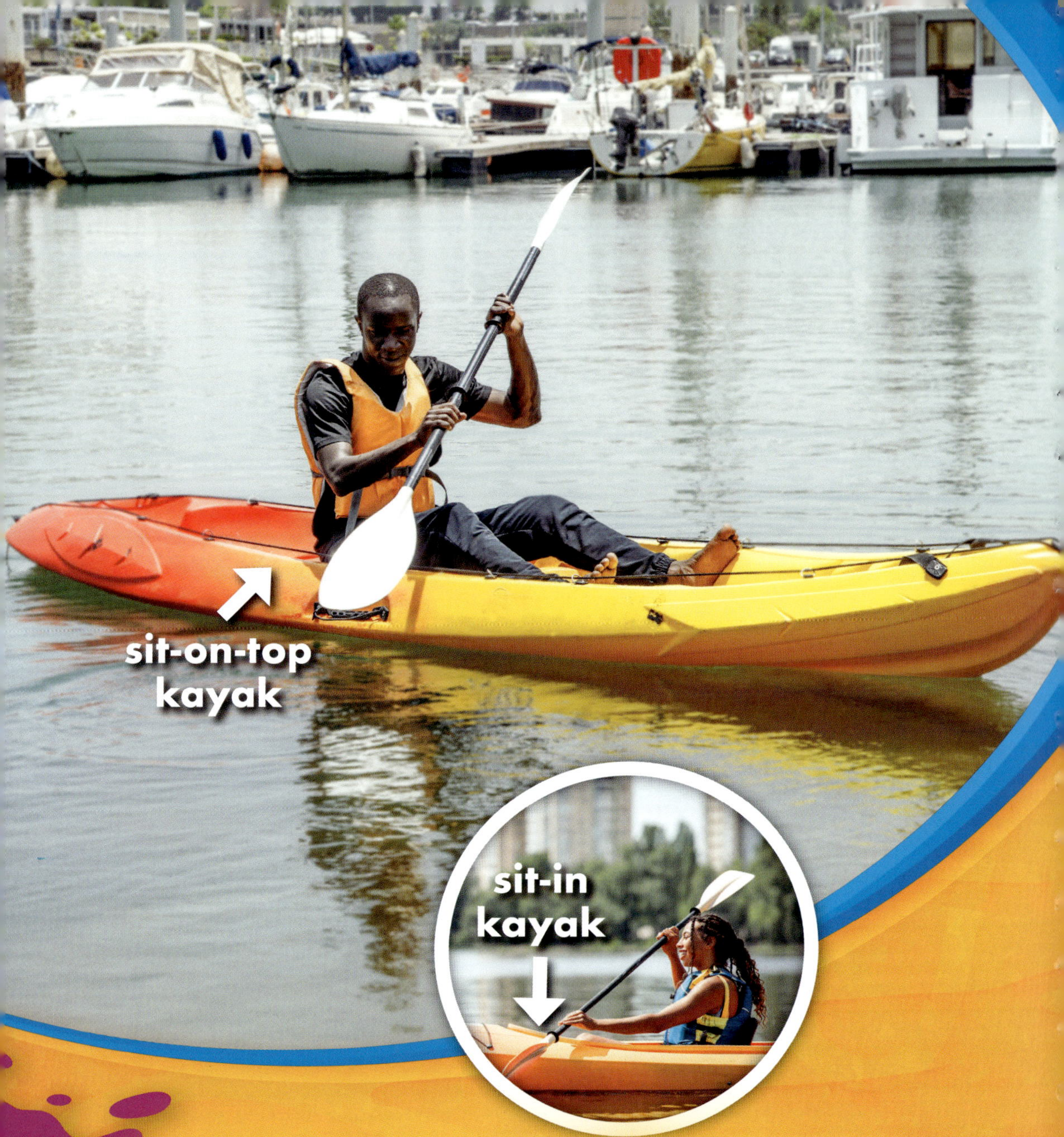

Sit-in kayaks have closed tops. Sit-on-top kayaks have open tops. They are easier for beginners.

Some kayaks can hold up to four people.

Kayakers use a **paddle** to move their kayaks. The paddles have **blades** on both ends.

Kayakers dress for the weather. They should wear a life jacket.

Kayakers pack important safety gear. They carry a whistle to blow for help.

They use a **bilge pump** to keep water out of their kayaks.

What Kayakers Need

Getting Started Kayaking

Kayaks come in different sizes.

Wide kayaks are better for beginners. Small kayakers use shorter kayaks.

Beginners get the feel for their kayaks onshore. They set the **foot pegs**.

They bend their knees slightly. Next, they **launch** the boat.

Kayakers **straddle** their kayaks in **shallow** water. They sit down in the **cockpit** and pull each leg inside.

They use their paddle to push off into deeper water.

To paddle, kayakers dip one blade into the water at a time.

How to Paddle

forward stroke

backward stroke

sweep stroke

draw stroke

They pull to move forward. They push to go backward. They sweep the paddle on one side to turn.

Go Paddle

Kayakers must know how to swim. Beginners should stay on **calm** water.

They should never go out alone. Go paddle in nature!

Glossary

bilge pump—a tool that removes water that collects in the bottom of a kayak

blades—wide, flat surfaces on paddles

bow—the front of a boat

calm—still and peaceful

cockpit—the seat of a kayak

foot pegs—flat objects to place feet against while paddling

launch—to move a boat into water

paddle—a tool used to move and steer a small boat

shallow—not deep

stern—the back of a boat

straddle—to stand or sit with one leg on either side of something

To Learn More

AT THE LIBRARY

Doeden, Matt. *White-water Kayaking*. Mankato, Minn.: Black Rabbit Books, 2024.

Grack, Rachel. *Rowing*. Minneapolis, Minn.: Bellwether Media, 2027.

Owings, Lisa. *Kayaking*. Minneapolis, Minn.: Bellwether Media, 2023.

ON THE WEB

FACTSURFER

Factsurfer.com gives you a safe, fun way to find more information.

1. Go to www.factsurfer.com.
2. Enter "kayaking" into the search box and click 🔍.
3. Select your book cover to see a list of related content.

Index

The images in this book are reproduced through the courtesy of: ARouchau, front cover (top); Dudarev Mikhail, front cover (bottom), p. 4; LIGHTFIELD STUDIOS, p. 3; Stratos Giannikos, pp. 4-5; Joe Sanders, p. 5; LightField Studios, p. 6; Hind Bouquartacha, pp. 6-7; Eachamoleks, p. 7; Wanwajee Weeraphukdee, p. 8; URAIWONS, pp. 8-9; Paul James, pp. 10-11; kazakova0684, p. 11 (life jacket); New Africa, p. 11 (kayak); marekuliasz, p. 11 (bilge pump); Refox Photos, p. 11 (paddle); Ward DeWitt, pp. 12-13; FamVeld, p. 13; isabela66, p. 14; Dmytro Sheremeta, pp. 14-15; SolStock, pp. 16-17, 18-19; Pierdelune, p. 17; Rodion Popov, p. 19 (forward stroke); Heliosphile, p. 19 (backward stroke); aapsky, p. 19 (sweep stroke); Vladimir Endovitskiy, p. 19 (draw stroke); JONGWI, pp. 20-21; Jayakri, p. 21; Artur Didyk, p. 23.